Stuffing Sandwiches Down My Shirt... Strategies and Inspiration for Crutch Users

HEATHER DUGAN

Stuffing Sandwiches Down My Shirt...

"Stuffing Sandwiches Down My Shirt... Strategies and Inspiration for Crutch Users"

An upbeat approach to one-footed living, this book delivers practical ideas for maximizing the temporary challenges associated with a casted leg and crutch use. The author, a single mom of three, found humor to be critical in making her post-op recovery time a fulfilling and, surprisingly, fun experience. Gym workouts, grocery shopping and even happy hours remained on the schedule. She deemed her cast to be "better than a puppy" in facilitating human connection.

"You will be inspired to put your 'best foot forward'..."

"'Sandwiches...' is all about attitude with a capital 'A'..."

Stuffing Sandwiches Down My Shirt...

REVIEWS:

"'Stuffing Sandwiches Down My Shirt...' is a very practical and inspirational look at how to survive and excel in recovering from an injury or in this case, surgery. Ms. Dugan uses her upbeat humor to share her own thoughts and creative solutions to the very real challenges encountered during recovery from surgery. She also shows how one can take ownership of their recovery and stay active in a safe and practical manner. As a surgeon, I will strongly recommend my patients to read this perspective BEFORE their procedure when possible so they can be as knowledgeable and proactive as possible. Thanks for sharing this perspective Heather!"

Dr Christopher Hyer, DPM
Westerville, Ohio

"Heather Dugan's 'Stuffing Sandwiches Down My Shirt...' is totally 'on spot' for anyone destined for a leg cast. It's also 'required reading' for those who think recuperating after any surgery is "just something to get through." Why? Because 'Sandwiches...' is all about attitude with a capital 'A'. Attitude makes the difference between 'waiting-for-it-to-be-over' and meeting the post-surgery challenge creatively 'armed' and with gusto.

Stuffing Sandwiches Down My Shirt...

Because Heather speaks from a very kind heart, 'Sandwiches...' is more than a DIY manual —it's as if Heather becomes your personal mentor urging you to adopt your own "yes, I can" attitude. We know 'Attitude' affects the healing process —so thank you, Heather, for such an enjoyable and health-enhancing read.

Monda Sue Prior, MSW, LICSW
Brewster, Massachusetts

"Heather Dugan's 'Stuffing Sandwiches Down My Shirt...' is really a great story about Heather's determination to not let a temporary setback like "walking on crutches" stop her from being happy, active and fit —mentally, emotionally and physically...

This book will take you on Heather's journey from the hopelessness of not being able to run again to her spirited triumph over the many obstacles in her way... You will be inspired to put your 'best foot forward' enthusiastically when faced with challenges. Bravo Heather!

Mark Dillworth, BA, PES
Austin, Texas

ALSO BY HEATHER DUGAN

PICKUP IN AISLE TWELVE

Stuffing Sandwiches Down My Shirt...

TABLE OF CONTENTS

Introduction 3
Prologue 7
My Story 13
Chapter 1: Five Critical Medical Lessons Learned 19
Chapter 2: Safety First 27
Chapter 3: Your Attitude 35
Chapter 4: Planning and Processes 45
Chapter 5: Enlisting Friends 57
Chapter 6: Strategies for Creating a Good
Experience 71
Chapter 7: Six Months Off the New Starting Line 83
More Inspiration:
Six More Upsides to My Downtime on Crutches 94
The Calendar Check 100
Donating Dreams and Gifts of Life:
Giving When it Hurts 104
Reader Letter: My Whole Life is Changing
Because of a Stupid Broken Foot 108
Reformed Gym Class Wallflower: Creating
Achievement Opportunities Instead of Excuses 112
About the Author 115
Other Books 119

Stuffing Sandwiches Down My Shirt...

DEDICATION

My deepest gratitude to Adrianne, Kelli, Sue, Eileen, Dawn, Dee, Bob, Dennis and my children Zak, Hannah and Matthew for their invaluable help and encouragement during my recovery and to my surgeon Dr. Christopher Hyer and physical therapists Liz and Brittany for their expert care.

And to those of you who have written in the midst of your own physical challenges, may this inspire you to press forward with the firm conviction that you, too, can journey back to health and healing.

Stuffing Sandwiches Down My Shirt...

INTRODUCTION

"Life will go on, with or without your active participation."

So your doctor said "surgery" or maybe you had an injury that required an unpleasant detour through a hospital emergency room, and now part of your leg has been tunneled into a hard fiberglass cast. Maybe it was your arm or hip or shoulder... Whatever the afflicted body part, wearing a cast will impact your whole life, full-time, for the duration of encasement. Making a color choice you can live with is the least of your worries (although, it's wise to choose a hue that will complement your seasonal shoe selection— neon green plays better on the color swatch ring than it will in business meetings). Retrofitting your life to accommodate a temporary handicap requires serious thought, planning and a *lot* of creativity.

While my experience has been with two separate lower leg casts, most of the principles I've discovered are applicable to many of our most difficult life experiences. Discouragement and depression, frustration and feelings of isolation can trail one home from the hospital unless you're prepared to launch yourself forward and out of their reach. Knowing the innate brevity of *life,* it seems wasteful to simply *endure* a few challenging weeks. Why not find ways to enjoy them as a unique and growing experience?

What will your approach be? Life will go on, with or without your active participation.

PROLOGUE

"Usually it's a sandwich. Wrapped, of course."

As I stuffed a Greek yogurt into my waistband, flinched at the sudden coldness, and took off on my crutches towards my study, it hit me: Very soon, I'm going to have to break some very effective but socially awkward habits!

Come to think of it, my friend Kelli burst out laughing while on her cell phone in my kitchen yesterday. I assumed her mom had said something funny. But her eyes were on the grocery list I was matter-of-factly stuffing down the front of my shirt.

Usually it's a sandwich. Wrapped, of course.

It's instinctive at this point. If I don't have my backpack handy, I become my own downsized UPS delivery system. Spoons slide into my leg cast, my cell phone peeks out of my bra. But I'm going to have to stop it, when I'm hands-free again. People give gentle leeway to the lady on crutches. Sticking mail down my pants at the curb without crutches propped against the mailbox will just look a little crazy. I need to prepare for this.

It took time to develop all my finely tuned shortcuts. I don't think twice about them now: Swinging like Tarzan's Jane into my shower, sipping wine from a transportable sports water bottle in the evening, spontaneously sticking my right leg out behind me in an arabesque or propping it up on a store shelf when numbness dictates that I elevate it —these are routine.

Frequently, I play with my toes to make sure they're still wiggling properly. I hop great distances on one foot (even further when I forget where I left my crutches). I fling things: rolls of toilet paper, bags of bagels, newspapers —slap-shotting them with a crutch when I miss my mark. When not engaged as transport, my right crutch does double-duty as an over-sized pointer and as the liberator of top shelf items beyond my grasp. *I've developed a deft "poke and duck" move.* I swing past people at the mall, calling, "passing on your left" to alert them to my precarious presence. Walls of people miraculously part for me. This is my new normal.

And while I hated to ask for help in the beginning, I've learned to accept and even expect that aid will be available. At the gym, I stand near a weight bench, make eye contact with a smile, and magically, assorted dumbbells appear at my feet. Friends carry my bags when we shop. They open doors for me, bring me food, napkins and drinks and stand as willing buffers lest I fall. For strenuous labor, this is actually pretty easy.

Being catered to as royalty could go to a girl's head — well maybe not the kind of girl who would also scoot down the stairs on her butt— but in four more weeks this extreme concierge service will finally come to an end.

I'm hoping I'll land back on both feet with continued gratitude and heightened understanding —and hoping that I can break my habit of stuffing my bra with household items. *Efficiency can be a bit addictive.*

MY STORY

"No wonder I was experiencing 'discomfort.'"

Let's just skip past the tedious, excruciating and slightly embarrassing details of my injury and begin just after I'd limped into the orthopedic exam room. My right ankle has never been an ally, but while I didn't expect a pat on the shoulder, I had hopes of a solution I could live with. When the surgeon finally appeared with an intern in tow, he opened with, "You aren't going to like this."

Mind reader. Yes, none of it was good. Holes in bones, messed up ligaments. No wonder I was experiencing "discomfort."

"Your running days are over," he stated before outlining his "fix," ankle fusion, which frankly, sounded less like a solution than it did a life sentence.

"Won't walking with a frozen ankle hurt my hip?"

It wasn't a long drop to "bottom." From that desolate place —a future with no running, limited hiking, flat uninspired footwear, a potential limp and accelerated arthritis in proximate joints —I *had* to get a grip. To allow this life limiting, permanent repair, I would have to be certain it was truly my only option.

It wasn't. While ankle fusion is considered "standard treatment" for my injury and relative youth, there were at least two immediately obvious alternate routes. I enlisted my aunt, and, together, we Googled new technologies, clinical trials, medical papers, forums and conference notes. I phoned and emailed doctors and nurses throughout the US and abroad. I sought out former patients —even speaking with a professional football player who kindly phoned me on his way to training practice. When attempting to get my insurance company to cover out-of-network surgery in New York as an in-network event proved fruitless ("*You can't seek medical authorization of your own surgery! I can't believe no one caught this before now!*"), and the Ohio Department of Insurance confirmed no successful appeals, I moved on and researched my in-network options again. By now, I was fairly knowledgeable of both my injuries and treatment options.

Finally some five months after that initial appointment, I scheduled surgery with another highly qualified surgeon whom I had grown to trust. *His* solution involved, in very simple terms, two bone grafts and a ligament graft. His aim was to repair my ankle and restore missing cartilage without shutting the door on future medical advancements.

As I write this, one week after the surgery (and my first real shower —heaven!), I'm thankful to be one-stepping it, with crutches, on the rebound road. I've seven more non-weight bearing, non-driving weeks, but this is manageable —especially when contrasted against the first medical solution offered me, which would have irretrievably diminished my life.

CHAPTER 1

This first chapter is for those individuals who have been advised of a need for surgery but have not yet undergone an actual procedure.

Stuffing Sandwiches Down My Shirt...

"Ultimately, you are in charge of what is done to your body. You get to take it home and live with the results."

FIVE CRITICAL LESSONS LEARNED

1) Your doctor is a problem solver seeking to fix your problem from his own personal set of tools. Don't assume he has researched the latest solutions for your particular issue or that he will seek out alternate ideas from respected colleagues. His aim is to repair your injury in a manner your insurance company is likely to cover.

Always, always, always seek a second or third opinion for major medical decisions. Yes, it may cost you a few co-pays, but pro-rate that money over the years ahead. You're paying for information that will impact the rest of your life, so price it accordingly. When examining long-term ramifications, how can you afford not to?

2) He's intelligent, but he doesn't have all the answers because the answers change all the time. Good doctors never stop learning, but they also have to treat enough patients to cover their exorbitant malpractice insurance.

Researchers and scientists progress our understanding of medical possibilities daily. Pair that with lightning fast advancements in technology, and no matter how committed a doctor may be it's almost impossible for him to keep completely current while also working a medical practice.

3) It is unlikely you will be given all your options, so you will have to do your own homework. Surf the Internet using keywords for your condition or injury. Get the correct medical terminology as well as the more patient-friendly terms for your issue(s). Search also the standard and alternative treatments. Chances are that one thing will lead to another and then on to another. Bookmark applicable websites and keep a text document of your search terms as you define them and the resources (people, organizations) you need to contact. Check for long-term results with each potential treatment. Will committing to one treatment now limit your options if it should fail? Look for both positive and negative outcomes other patients have experienced. Seek to understand worst case and best-case scenarios so that you can properly evaluate your risks.

4) You may offend a doctor (or two, if you're me), but that's OK. It's *your* life. Would you politely stand by while a helpful bystander attempted to swat a mosquito off your head with a hammer? Of course not. Be respectful. Be appreciative —your doctor has put in years of study and experience. But own it. Ultimately, you are in charge of what is done to your body. You get to take it home and live with the results. It's OK to say "no" or "I need to think about this" or "I'd like to get a third opinion." Ask about success rates, probably outcomes, and if there is anything you personally can do to enhance your recovery.

Sometimes it won't work out. Bad chemistry happens in business and in dating. It also occurs with medical professionals. Be kind and courteous, but don't sacrifice your health for the sake of social niceties.

5) Be prepared to wait on your best option because a "quick fix" may be costly. The first time I underwent ankle surgery ten years ago, I had three young children and couldn't bear the thought of being laid up for any length of time. I wanted to get it over with and scheduled surgery with the first recommended surgeon. That worked out OK, I guess. I'll never know if I might have had better results because in my hurry to reach a "fix," I failed to investigate all available methods (and surgeons) to achieve it.

There are true emergency situations where your only choice is immediate medical action. But most of the time, you *have* time. See if there is a way to stabilize your situation while you investigate your choices. This time, I used crutches and even my old surgical walking boot as needed. I wore an athletic brace for a Colorado hiking trip with my kids and stepped carefully through the snowfields (What was I going to do? Mess up my ankle?). When I was finally comfortable that I'd found the right solution for me, I scheduled the surgery for the first available date after my kids' fall sports seasons ended. No, there is never a convenient time for a single self-employed mom to have surgery, but there are times that are less horrible. I aimed for one of those.

So… seven weeks to go until I can push a gas pedal or walk with both feet. That's a lot of time to learn a few more things! My pre-surgery time and "week one" have been challenging and enlightening.

I'll be sharing what I learn on this journey in hopes it will save you a step or two.

That was a joke. The "step or two" part.

CHAPTER 2

"Safety demands that you be confident in your choices."

SAFETY FIRST

If it "went without saying," I wouldn't be saying it. Follow the rules. Those sheets of paper the nurse sent home with your designated driver are your roadmap during the first few days of recovery. Do not deviate from the charted course without a clear understanding of the potential consequences!

Your instructions are bound to include a few basics like rest, icing, elevating, keeping the cast dry, pain management and hydration.

Icing and elevating your wrapped limb will make a huge difference in both your final result and your recovery time. Rest is essential for at least the first couple of days. And don't be a hero on the pain pills —when your nurse advises you to keep "ahead" of the pain, listen.

Be good to yourself by A) Defining acceptable activity boundaries with your doctor or surgical assistant, B) Following the rules (really, I mean this) and C) Avoiding spontaneous choices. Pretend your casted leg is your unborn baby —protect it. The undercover healing that is happening beneath your cast needs all the nurturing care that a growing infant does. Good nutrition, safe levels of exercise and following doctor's orders are part of the deal, so try to be a good patient.

Yes, I'm the one who managed to lock myself out of the house during an impromptu crutch walk three days after my surgery. And I have a tendency to call out "passing on your left" as I swing past laggards at the mall or grocery. But I like to focus on a good choice I recently made:

My friend Dawn and I were running a couple "get Heather out of the house" errands at an indoor mall near my home. She had flinched and flung arms a few times to protect me from unobservant Christmas shoppers. And I probably didn't help her heart rate with my rapid pace (crutches are an excellent cardio workout). When we found ourselves a floor above for our final stop, I matter-of-factly approached the escalator. I had already managed a couple of rides earlier in the week and was determined to meet all challenges before me.

Poor Dawn. "There's an elevator right there!" She motioned towards the golden doors fifty feet beyond us as enthusiastically as she might a good boot sale. I smiled at her and continued toward the escalator.

"There's an elevator over there, Heather!" She had decided I didn't hear her and repeated herself two more times, her tone rising in alarm.

I waited for her to catch up to me at the top of the busy escalator. "I can do this."

"There's an elevator…" Her voice trailed off. "Then I'm going first. Unless you want to try the elevator?"

I laughed, and she smiled resignedly. Shaking her head at me, Dawn stepped on to the moving steps, bracing herself to catch me if I fell forward.

Confidently, I swung up on my crutches —and then promptly froze. At that moment, I had no idea what motion came next. I struggled to remember what I had done just a day before while Dawn frantically scrambled up the steps to maintain a space directly in front of me. As she began to drift (and gamely kept trying, I must add), I finally had to acknowledge my stubbornness. "Never mind, I'll take the stupid elevator!"

It felt like a minor defeat to meekly join the mothers with strollers in the elevator a moment later, but as I replayed the moment in my mind, I knew I'd made the right choice. When experiencing hesitation on crutches, it is foolish to take an unplanned action. Safety demands that you be confident in your choices.

And I did get my escalator ride in the opposite direction moments later after we found that our targeted store had "misplaced" itself yet again at the other end of the level we'd just left.

* Always carry a charged cell phone, and always let someone know when you plan to do something out of the ordinary (whether retrieving something from your basement or taking a crutch walk down your street).

CHAPTER 3

"My cast is better than a puppy."

YOUR ATTITUDE

From TIPS FROM THE TIGHTROPE *"It's Not a Crutch if it Makes You Stronger: 8 Weeks, 9 Discoveries:"*

There is nothing dignified about slinging a backpack over your fluffy pink bathrobe and trekking to breakfast in your own kitchen. But it could be worse…

It helps to remember that.

Because this is familiar, schlepping about on crutches with a surgically repaired ankle. The last ankle imposition occurred ten years ago to the same right foot that would typically be pressing a gas pedal to get my body to the grocery, the gym and, basically, "my life." Now encased in a burgundy Christmas stocking of a cast (that works nicely with either a brown or black boot, BTW), it's getting no action for eight weeks. No walking, driving or cooking until sometime in January. *I added the "no cooking" part myself.*

Last time, the temporary wing clipping challenged my spirit. Anything "fun" required planning. The leg cast killed spontaneous choices. Out of coffee? Out of luck.

I knew this second surgery would be more difficult. During my first procedure and recovery, I'd had some in-home help from my now ex-husband. This time I would face it as a single self-employed mom with more responsibilities than I could juggle when deftly balanced on two feet. I foresaw a lot of dropped balls with a one-footed lifestyle.

As the hospital date neared, panic crept in. I began "nesting" in the manner of a pregnant mom preparing for the arrival of her baby. Instead of repainting a nursery, I worried about burnt out light bulbs, throw rugs, the furnace filter and car maintenance —not that my car would be going anywhere for a while. I made vegetable soup, washed towels and swept out my garage. It was "busy work," but since de-stressing with a trail run was out and screaming might damage my vocal chords, I dusted.

Two weeks in, and I'm somewhat shocked to find it's not that bad. Yes, there are inconveniences, but now that I can swing into the shower to wash my hair and have figured out how to feed my dog and make coffee without fainting —it's manageable. And I've only locked myself out of the house once.

And actually, there are some things I *like* about this mandatory challenge. Strange? I agree. Let me explain...

1) I am more focused. Traipsing into a room only to spin in circles trying to remember why I headed there in the first place is out of the question now. First off, there is no "traipsing" on crutches. *After dark, I've been compared to a one-legged pirate who could easily manage the sound effects for a B-grade horror flick.* Spinning? On my butt, maybe… But the biggest difference is that when I'm aimed at the kitchen or my office, I firmly remember my intent with every plant of the crutches. It may take me a little longer to arrive, but I bet I'm back out the door in less time overall. Physical labor tends to keep one in the moment.

2) I am more organized. Before I head to record audio for my clients or to my kitchen for breakfast, I load up my backpack with an iPad, water bottle, phone and apple (the professional's trick for clearer sounding voiceovers). Before I settle in for my daily thirty-minute session with my Magnetic Bone Stimulator, I assemble writing projects, phone contacts and make sure my bedroom shade is open to the woods behind my house. When I had the luxury of walking back and forth to a room as I remembered additional needs, I made multiple trips. Without the two-step option, I do it all in one.

3) I have become a better planner. Making meals, getting the mail, feeding my dog… My mind is now forced to break down basic tasks into the individual steps that are least likely to require calling my surgeon's assistant with an "oops" message. Swinging out of the shower (with my leg encased in a really nifty

Dry Pro Waterproof Cast Cover) requires creating an absorbent landing spot for my good foot and a non-skid surface for my crutches. Grocery shopping is now an "outing," and I'm less likely to forget the blueberry bagels. I don't foresee completely losing my tendency toward spontaneity, but let's just say it's less of a crutch. *Smile. That was a joke.*

4) I'm a creative problem-solver. It's actually kind of fun to figure out how I'm going to transport a cup of Greek yogurt to my office or the contents of my bathroom hamper to the laundry room. By viewing tasks as puzzles to be solved, they become less of a problem and more of a challenge. I like challenges.

One safety tip? Aim to do the more challenging one-legged tasks in a corner where you'll have more surface area to fall against if you misjudge your abilities. Toss what won't break —an excellent way to move a packaged roll of paper towels, for instance. Carry everything else in a plastic grocery bag, backpack or down your shirt if necessary. *Creativity isn't always an artistically beautiful experience.*

5) I'm spending more time with friends and deepening those relationships. While my initial days on Percocet provided humorous anecdotes (wiggling my nerve-blocked toes and remembering the names of medical personnel was apparently very important to me), opening my unkempt home and awkward self to others adds a new and nervy dimension to "keeping it real." I'm less likely to apologize for dust now. It's not that I spent a lot of time dusting before, but I care a lot less about that particular failing now. And nobody else really cared to begin with. Friends and even work colleagues are forced to either visit me at home or pick me up for get-togethers. Getting up and down steps can be a bonding experience, and I've only kneed one male friend in the groin so far.

6) My cast is better than a puppy. It's an eye catcher and an icebreaker. In fact, my single girlfriends are interested in testing its residual effects on men *they* might want to meet. And it's not just a male/female thing. People of all ages and both genders gravitate to the poor lady with the leg cast. Many elderly folks can relate to my limitations. Fascinated children reserved me a special place at the Thanksgiving dinner table. I'd love to see what doors this cast could kick open on a trip to Europe or Asia.

7) I found my "pause" button. Well, that was temporary, but there were a few days where I was forced to simply wait. We all need that experience from time to time. It's a "reset." That rest period built my resolve and energy levels to effectively meet the challenges of daily living as I move through my recovery.

8) I am more grateful. I'm pretty big on living with gratitude as it is, but my appreciation for the kindnesses of family and friends and my enjoyment for the simple pleasures of crutch-walking down my street or dining out with friends has grown.

More gratitude = more joy. This terrible and inconvenient surgery has actually enhanced what is good in my life!

9) Here's the big one. In texting with a kindred spirit/friend the other night, I finally pinpointed the game changer in this experience. While I dragged my heels all the way to the hospital and spent a couple of foggy days on pain killers immediately following the surgery, at some point on the third day I adjusted my view of the traumatic event. **This is no longer something to "get through" but is rather another accomplishment I can achieve.**

Coincidentally, I think that was the same day I let my dog out the garage door, got a sudden craving for Greek yogurt located in the outside fridge, noticed that it was a beautiful sunny day and proceeded to take my first walk, locking myself out of the house in the process. Still in my initial post-op splint, I made my way to a neighbor's front porch and giggled at her horrified expression at finding me there. She helped me find my key and get back into my home to where I could again dutifully elevate my leg.

The eight weeks ahead didn't look any easier, but my perspective was changed. This is no vacation, but I now recognize this to be an eight-week experience I'm unlikely to repeat —and it's an opportunity to succeed at some new challenges. Ironically, with this cast on my foot and these crutches at my side, I feel stronger than ever.

*The single biggest thing you can do to enhance your healing process, besides following your doctor's "rules," is to grip onto a positive attitude with both hands. It will slip from your grasp occasionally. After one of my few truly "cooped up in the house" days, a simple "how are you doing?" from my cousin Holly sent me into tearful sobs. But it was honest, she had the time to listen, and I found myself completely reenergized for the challenges of the next morning. There were also a few times that getting myself ready for a big day loomed as an Everest-sized hurdle. Taking a couple of deep breaths and reminding myself that I was capable of each single task allowed me to take first steps that rolled into full accomplishments.

Also, I learned to temporarily lower my house cleanliness standards. Healing my body was more important than facing off against dust bunnies!

CHAPTER 4

Stuffing Sandwiches Down My Shirt...

"Establishing each step of the process ahead of
time... made it less likely I'd make an error that
would harm me."

PLANNING AND PROCESSES

Doing laundry, making coffee, taking a shower… these normally easy tasks are now multistep processes. There will be some things that are simply too dangerous to your recovery, and you will have to find help. *If you lock yourself out of the house, I recommend my next-door neighbor who does a great look of horror for post-op patients appearing on her doorstep with splint and crutches.*

Some of these challenges will be readily evident to you pre-surgery. Many will surprise you. Daily habits such as reading the paper with your morning cup of coffee may become small luxuries. But with a little forethought, many or most tasks can still be accomplished.

One of my most useful items was my hiking backpack for easy transport of my essentials throughout the house, the gym and on errands. Yes, it feels a little silly to wear a backpack over your bathrobe in the morning —but I chose to view it as an empowering, and therefore attractive, accessory. And a bathrobe with pockets —in fact any garment with pockets— will provide even more carrying capacity and flexibility.

Here's a short list of items that made it into my backpack: Water bottle, iPad, laptop, phone, bills, reminder notes, books, jackets, bagged or packaged food (cheese, pretzels, fruit/veggies, sandwiches,

Greek yogurt with spoon), newspapers, mail, moisturizer, paper towels, wine bottle, wine glass, corkscrew… Viewing my temporary handicap as a virtual camping trip in my own home, made it more palatable. Yes, there were times I wanted something other than a sandwich for lunch, but I determined early on to be a good "happy-to-be-fed" camper, which made daily life infinitely more enjoyable. Using the backpack made it less of an exercise in minimalism.

Tight-sealing water bottles are invaluable. It's important to remain well hydrated during your recovery, particularly while on medications and exercising at the higher intensity that goes with crutches use. My *gym* water bottle became my 24/7 *around-the-house* water bottle.

Plastic grocery bags, also, were useful for carrying everything from the mail to dirty laundry. I kept a couple in my backpack and secreted others at strategic points throughout the house.

Duplication made things easier. Two water bottles proved better than one. I left pens and index cards for list making at multiple locations as well.

In the beginning, I had to retrace my steps a few times before I learned to breakdown tasks into achievable pieces. Eventually, I learned to plan ahead: If I had audio to record, I loaded my backpack with my water bottle, my iPad (loaded with the relevant scripts), a paper towel-wrapped apple (for cleaner voice sound) and my silenced phone before I retreated to my recording closet.

When I was finally allowed to take a real one-legged shower, I thought through each step beforehand. With no backup in the house, it was vital that there be no surprises that could allow injury and impact my recovery. Dry cast protector in place, I was able to safely swing into the shower, accomplish my cleansing and swing back out, taking care to land my good foot onto a bath mat. Crutches propped nearby, I made sure to plant them on the tile, rather than the rug, when I was ready to move back toward my bedroom. Establishing each step of the process ahead of time, such as the importance of placing my wet foot on the bathmat and my dry crutches onto the tile, made it less likely I'd make an error that would harm me.

This step-by-step approach is how I approached each task: gathering mail, feeding my dog, doing laundry and making meals. Each task had to be broken down into a series of things I knew that I could do to avoid any risk to my healing ankle. Thinking through the necessary steps also gave me more confidence, which added to my success.

Let's break down two simple tasks you will almost certainly need to handle.

Daily Grooming at the Sink (before you're able to use the shower):

1) Assemble supplies: Planning is the hardest part of this, because forgetting items is burdensome in the beginning (but it gets easier). You may want to gather shampoo, conditioner, a comb, towel, washcloth, soap, deodorant, toothpaste, toothbrush, razor, shaving cream, lotion, blow dryer, moisturizer, makeup, cell phone (always have one handy in case you need help!) and a chair.

You will help yourself by creating one-stop stations for yourself —at your sink, in the kitchen, at the gym… Plan to do as much as possible in one place.

2) Consider the most efficient order in which you can do your tasks: Forget your usual routine. What makes sense *now* when your leg —or arm— is in a cast? Your plan should be to accomplish your daily hygiene as efficiently as possible, resting on the chair as needed. And make sure there is leaning space on your countertop! In the beginning, you will fatigue easily. Hopefully, you will have some help. But if you don't —and I didn't— it's still possible to avoid the disheveled damsel-in-distress (or dude-in-disarray) look.

3) Plan for your injured limb. It wasn't pretty. While washing my hair (and grocery shopping, crutch walking, talking with friends…), I often had to do impromptu arabesques to elevate my leg. It was fairly easy to tip it up while washing my hair in the sink, but not such an elegant move at other times. Yes, I even stuck it on the edge of store shelves and trashcans when necessary. Because I had gone through an earlier ankle surgery, I was very aware of the importance of elevating my leg with the first throbbing sensation. If you have a casted arm, it may make sense to pile towels on one side of the sink so that you can rest it as you rinse your hair.

4) Be efficient. If you condition your hair, why not use that time to shave whatever you can while sitting on the chair? Others may deem that frivolous, but for me, shaving what parts of my legs I could reach made me feel human, so I did that for me. In that first splinted post-op week, I spent more time sitting on the chair than standing at the sink, but towards the end of the week, I found I was able to do a few leg lifts while resting —and it continued to get better from there.

5) Don't underestimate the energy expense. Getting ready for the day usually wiped me out for a few minutes. So, I made sure I was fueled with food before starting and then retreated to my bed immediately afterward to elevate my foot and tap away on my laptop —and ice my ankle.

I cannot stress enough how much you will help yourself by icing your surgical site regularly. Help yourself heal —ice and elevate!

Making Meals:

1) Keep it simple to enable success. In the beginning, there was no morning coffee. And frankly, while on Percocet the first few days, I didn't miss it at all —zzzzz... Friends and my kids kept me well-nourished much of the time, but I usually had to figure out at least a couple of meals on my own. In the beginning, absent any help, warm soup was simply not an option: I remember standing in front of my elevated microwave oven, considering it. Sensibly, I decided the risk of scalding myself while precariously balanced on one foot would make for a rather embarrassing 911 call.

2) Bend a little. Omelet assembly was impractical on one foot —*and I'm better at eating them than making them anyway.* But I figured I could toast a breakfast bagel, so that was my first solo breakfast. I made the same kinds of choices for lunch. While soup often sounded good on a cold winter day, I learned to be happy with a warmed sandwich instead. Plates were breakable unless carefully slid across countertops, so I often wrapped food in paper towels and either stuffed them down my shirt or stuck them in my backpack.

3) Throw things. In the beginning you might be tempted to simply throw tantrums, and if you need to scream occasionally, have at it. But tossing boxes of cereal, bags of bagels… basically enclosed *anything*… is often smarter than attempting a crutches carry. So have fun with it. *Do* lean on something for support for your first few tosses. As you grow more proficient, the crutch on the side of your injured leg can be great for poking, pushing and prodding items around the house —*and nudging slow or irritating people as well.*

4) Find your "workarounds." With a backpack and/or plastic grocery bag, your food transportation options open up tremendously. *Be careful not to put anything weighty into a carried bag, however. By your third or fourth crutch step, heavier items will develop a swing that will interfere with your balance. No need to risk a fall —use the backpack instead.* I found I could heat food in my microwave by leaning against the range to unseal the lid for heating and then to reseal it for careful placement in the backpack (or, as I got more advanced, I mastered a pivot/swivel maneuver to slide food to the kitchen island. Still no soup, though —I decided I wasn't up for making any messes I couldn't easily clean up myself).

Maybe you'd like to watch a movie or work on your laptop while sipping a glass of wine in the evening? I did. Crackers and cheese and a couple of napkins went into sealed bags in the backpack, as did my sports water bottle (which went everywhere I did). And I found I could still slip a wine bottle and glass in there as well... When I got to my bedroom "writing chaise," I unloaded my backpack onto the adjacent shelf and retrieved my laptop, if necessary, stowing it in the now emptied backpack. It wasn't that hard to accomplish and turned solo evenings into relaxed and productive nights.

5) Don't forget to hydrate. By the time you gather food, it's easy to decide you'll just drink milk (calcium!) or water later. Better to take the extra few minutes to include fluid with your meal —something *always* comes up "later," or you may get comfortably situated and lose the motivation to follow through on your good intention.

6) Consider supplements. Ask your doctor about your nutritional needs during the healing process. Extra protein, calcium and vitamin D may help your body in restoring bone health. And your calorie expenditure may be *much* higher if on crutches —mine was —so be sure to keep your energy and strength up by accommodating your body's additional needs.

CHAPTER 5

"Open a window and toss your pride out for now. You're better off without it while you're wearing that lovely hospital gown anyway... But it will get better."

ENLISTING FRIENDS

This quite frankly was the hardest part. Maybe you already pay someone to cut your grass or to tidy your home. Certainly, you're accustomed to compensating a waitress or waiter when they deliver food and drink to your dining table. So… how do you garner and accept help from people when you have no real idea of how repayment might be possible?

It's a cliff jump. For those of us used to paying our way up front, this will be very uncomfortable. Basically, you must leap into indebtedness with no coins in your pocket. Undoubtedly, there will be a repayment of sorts, but you have no way of knowing if you will repay favors directly back to the individuals who will be assisting you —or if you will be bestowing kindnesses upon individuals yet unknown to you. It would be easier to simply pay money or trade favor for favor in a directly quantifiable fashion, but this time, my friend, *you* are the charity case.

Ow. That's tough for most of us to manage. It implies a lack of control and an overabundance of need. Which is just about "spot on" when you're facing a surgical recovery. You may have to view yourself a little differently. Not as less capable —certainly not — but as someone who needs a bit of help to *be* fully capable for a temporary period of time. I know. This is hard! Open a window and toss your pride out for now.

You're better off without it while you're wearing that lovely hospital gown anyway, and you won't need it when you're groaning for pain meds either. But it will get better…

Oh, of course, Sarah/Jim/Amy/Drew will want to help me… but do I really have to ask?!

Yes, you do. They may be your dearest friends —or they may even be barest acquaintances —but they can't begin to guess what you need unless it is clearly communicated. And recovering from major surgery is no solo endeavor. Attempting to handle it in lone ranger fashion will jeopardize your recovery.

I'm just basically asking for endless favors?!

Well, yes. Basically. And the more people you ask, the less you will have to ask of each individual, so if you're the least bit worried about burdening others, it will pay to spread a wide net on his one.

If you're fortunate enough to have a spouse or close family members available, quit your whining. You're far ahead of where I was at post-op. But let that give you some assurance —if I, a single mom, could find the assistance I needed, you will too.

Plan ahead, starting with the surgery itself. You'll need drivers and possibly someone to wait while you undergo your procedure. Do you have a dog?

Children? A lawn that will need trimmed or a driveway that may require snow shoveling?

I don't mention these things to alarm you, but rather, hopefully, to spark your problem-solving capabilities. You won't think of everything —I can virtually guarantee that. You'll have to think on your feet — *er... foot*— a bit.

This is no complete list, but hopefully it will allow you to do some advance planning of your own for your surgery and recovery period.

Pre-Surgery:

Arrange transportation for yourself and any school-aged children.

Arrange pet care.

Ask your surgeon's office about what sort of care you may need in your first post-op days. Pick up any medications in advance if possible.

Stock up at the grocery store one last time.

Survey your home for potential hazards and, as much as possible, **arrange daily health and grooming essentials** so that you will be able to access them more easily. Take a minute to put shampoo, conditioner, a razor and washcloth/towel where you will be able to access them for that first sink washing session (you will most likely have to wait a few days for your first glorious shower).

Plan clothing and footwear options. It's so much easier to figure out the basics beforehand on two feet. Summertime? Easy. I wore shorts, skirts and either a tennis shoe or strapped sandal on my good left foot (no flip flops!). Winter was slightly more challenging, but the thought of spending eight weeks in gym pants was depressing, so I determined to upgrade on that. Assume you will *not* be able to fit jeans or most pants over a leg cast. I managed jeans once, but it was enough of an effort that I didn't repeat it. I found that a knee length skirt and a tall riding boot allowed me to move freely and avoid that "I'm a pitiful patient" look. To prevent my left boots getting noticeably worn over their closeted right foot counterparts, I encouraged my daughter to borrow my footwear and enable more even wear.

Here's what you *don't* do: Wanting to wear a short boot and *not* wanting to dissect any of my tights, I decided I could tie off the unused tight leg around the thigh of my casted leg. *Don't think too hard. Didn't really make sense.* I was pretty proud, both of my inventiveness and thriftiness until I discovered a black appendage dangling from beneath my skirt and between my legs. *Don't think about that either, although my friends found it rather funny.* I fixed it with a tighter tie off, almost cutting off my circulation, and later on, *still* found myself looking for a private corner in a *very* public place where I could yank up tights that were making a rapid descent down my good leg. Lesson learned: Cut 'em or don't bother wearing them.

Guys? I can't give you specific suggestions beyond a general "thumbs down" on the skirt idea. Hopefully, you have some slacks that are cut generously enough to accommodate a leg cast. If not, go buy some inexpensive pants you won't mind slicing to fit.

Call your insurance company to ascertain coverage of medical supplies. Using their preferred providers will save you money. And if a friend has crutches adjustable to your size, borrow them (and practice!) ahead of time. You may find it less expensive to obtain other medical devices (crutches, knee scooter…) ahead of time per your insurance company's policies. If you will be wearing a cast, procure a Dry Pro Waterproof Cast Cover for showering, swimming (and even walks in the rain).

Prepay monthly bills especially if you have no spouse or significant other. It's no fun fumbling through old paperwork when you have all those lovely new medical bills rolling in.

If possible, **arrange for a house cleaning and laundry catch-up day**. These tasks will be out of reach for a short while. Failing that, unscrew light bulbs and try to ignore the dust. Your healing will be the bigger priority.

Consider car service and home maintenance needs. I considered… and put most of them off. But typing a car service appointment onto my calendar for when I would again be mobile helped me feel a little more in charge of my life.

Schedule any needed hair, dental and medical appointments ahead of surgery if possible. I didn't put these off, knowing that desperate times can lead to desperate DIY haircuts.

Yes, there will be more. You will forget things but somehow manage to get through anyways.

Really! You will get through this!

My biggest initial mistake: I didn't consider how difficult it would be to care for my sweet but assertive chocolate lab Lily, and my last ditch effort to send her on a short "vacation" to my ex's fell through. On the third morning after my surgery, I found myself alone and on Percocet with a hungry and insistent dog-child to care for. That morning I made my second big mistake by trying to feed her first —a direct violation of the airline video "put the mask on your own self first" rule. I began to black out while crossing my kitchen tile on crutches and did an emergency lie-down. Thankfully, I didn't knock myself out or damage my doctor's good work on my ankle by crashing to the floor, but it was close. A few minutes rest allowed my body to recover enough that I could make my way to a box of crackers in the pantry, and with food, I was physically stable again. On most days after that, my youngest son was able to feed her. On the mornings he was at his dad's I took care to feed myself first and had no more fainting issues.

Tip: At random moments throughout your day, visualize doing a present task with a casted limb. What will you need to arrange or change ahead of time to enable your success?

After Your Surgery:

Say "yes, please" and "thank you." Accept offers of help with gratitude. You need help. No "poor me" is necessary. Hopefully, the giving and receiving of help can be a positive experience for both sides.

Plan and ask ahead. My friends usually tossed me a blanket "is there anything else you need" before leaving. I tried to genuinely consider that question each time it was asked, because, for instance, it was generally faster and safer for someone else to retrieve something from my basement than for me to bump down the steps myself.

My kids made a point of replenishing my ice cooler (to treat post-op swelling) before leaving the house for school or their dad's place. Had it been left for me to accomplish, I'd have had to scoot the length of my house pushing the cooler with my good leg —it was much easier confining my inelegant butt scooting to the master bath!

Offer options. You don't want to bother anyone. Yep, I get that. And some friends will have a sympathetic desire to assist but not know how to be helpful, so here are some strategies for avoiding the "great imposition."

1) Group text/email some of your requests. "I'm texting a few of you to see who might be available to get me to next Wednesday's doctor appointment at 10AM." By stating your need in this manner, it's less of a pressure and more of an opportunity. Also, try to set appointment times for when your friends are more likely to be available. Accommodate their schedules over your own desires.

2) Have a ready "laundry list." *Thanks for asking! Well... I'll need to get to the grocery and bank sometime in the next couple of days, my dog needs a walk, Tuesday is "trash day" and I'd love a ride to the gym sometime. Do you think you could help me with any one of those?"* Offering choices lets people help in more convenient ways. I found this to make the asking less stressful.

3) Take turns. Friends may be inclined to make it all about you. Try to avoid this. See if some of their own errands and shopping can be included in any outings. You're bound to learn something useful and might discover a new "favorite" by venturing further into their worlds. Adrianne took me to her favorite burger joint —somewhere I probably wouldn't have ever thought to go on my own —*and then teased me mercilessly for ordering a veggie sandwich.*

4) Enjoy the connection time. This is a chance to get to know one another within a new context. You will most likely get to problem solve together and will almost certainly grow a new level of intimacy. I remember a LOT of laughing as friends helped me in and out of my house, into their cars and out to accomplish necessary errands. We added lunch or dinner out when possible. When my friend Dee arrived to walk my dog, I often crutch-walked with her for at least part of Lily's exercise time so that we could enjoy some conversation time too.

5) Be humble. My first few drops into Adrianne's passenger seat were less than graceful. I basically fell backward onto her seat and prayed my skirt wouldn't catch a lofting breeze. I stumbled into Bob going down my garage steps and asked another friend to just carry me into my sofa one time early on when I wasn't yet confident of my ability to safely navigate steps — *probably soon after I fell into Bob!* It only took a week or two to gain proficiency, but it's important to keep your confidence in line with your abilities to avoid further injury. My friend Kelli, who had recently undergone a similar surgery, had lots of great suggestions —I listened and learned.

Stuffing Sandwiches Down My Shirt...

CHAPTER 6

Stuffing Sandwiches Down My Shirt...

"Retain your spot in life."

STRATEGIES FOR CREATING A GOOD EXPERIENCE

Whether or not you will retain driving privileges and a bit of independence, six to eight weeks of non-weight bearing living can be overwhelming. Similarly, multiple weeks with an incapacitated arm or shoulder can intimidate. And then comes physical therapy and rehabilitation…

It's a lot. These are not optional surgeries. Few would choose to live in such a semi-dependent state. Choices are relegated to our responses to this set of circumstances we really can't change.

But these are powerful choices…

1) Find a way to incorporate little luxuries. Your list will be different from mine, but two of my normalizing luxuries are a made-up bed and a pedicure. So, as soon as allowed, I painted my toenails a lovely pinkish purple and hopped around my king-sized bed to pull up the sheets and comforter every morning. These two things mattered to nobody but me. But because I knew they would make me feel better, I did them faithfully as a gift to myself.

You will have to let go of many of your customary pleasures. Instead of reflexively reaching for *all* of the things to which you're accustomed and facing frequent disappointment, pick a few significant luxuries that are maintainable to your lifestyle. Maybe it will be a daily phone call with a favorite friend, a bedside bouquet or favorite TV show. Your routine will change dramatically after a surgery, so stick a few of your favorite things into the schedule so that your daily experience will still resemble *your* life.

2) Maintain social connection. Isolation paired with physical limitation is depressing. Since you can't do much to shorten the limitation stage of your situation, make it a point to shift out of the isolation trap.

Phone calls, emails and texting are fine, but you will need face-to-face time. You will also need to change your environment by getting out of the house. So plan for it. Be assertive. Many will assume you need to lie in your bed and recover. This is most likely *not* the case and could actually hinder your comeback. When friends offered to run errands for me, I unabashedly begged to come along.

Retain your spot in life by participating. So you're on crutches, in a wheelchair or using a knee walker... Those are mechanical changes. They needn't create an emotional drain, because you can *and should* view them simply as new parameters from which you must temporarily navigate.

Here's my shortlist of activities enjoyed while on crutches: meals with friends, dinner dates, crutch walks in pouring rain (wearing my cast cover), grocery shopping, Christmas shopping, dog walking, almost daily trips to the gym, meetings with work colleagues, studio recording, dress shopping, business networking... Really, I did everything I would normally do except for impact activities and driving. Not so bad! And, I had friends dropping in (often with food) every day. I think I felt more loved and cared for in those weeks than I had in years!

Yes, I gave my friend Adrianne a slight panic when I attempted to balance on one foot while holding both food and drink at a Christmas party —*I promised to sit while imbibing thereafter.* Kelli, being similarly motivated on fitness goals, indulged my desire to *not* be dropped off at the grocery entrance, understanding my need to crutch walk my way across the parking lot *with* her. Eileen, Anna, Sandra and Dennis all kept me out in the world, hauling me to happy hours and business networking events. My out-of-state cousins and aunts kept in touch by phone (and my aunt even flew in to help me for a few days). It still amazes me that it worked out. With the first realization that a surgery would be necessary, I felt overwhelmed. But all of my fears —for my children, my business and my own mental health— proved unfounded. In retrospect, those weeks on crutches were the best part of my year.

3) Maintain physical activity. Focusing on the "no"s will be deflating, so instead seek out what you are still able to do. When your doctor tells you certain activities will be off limits, find out why. The two of you may be able to find a work-around or substitute.

Throughout my recovery, I did all I could to maintain strength while still protecting my casted leg. I chose to use crutches rather than a rolling knee walker, knowing that it would provide me better exercise. I crutch-walked my street with the intent of breaking a sweat. *My kids insisted on accompanying me after I locked myself out the one time.* I did leg lifts, crunches, stretching, one-legged pushups, pull-ups at the gym and weight work. By keeping myself active, I was ready for rehab when that blessed start date finally arrived.

Keeping myself active kept me hopeful and positively focused, because everyday I was proving myself to be capable. That was a powerful message to communicate to myself, and it had a positive impact on both my mental attitude and my recovery speed.

For fun, one day at the gym, my friend Kelli and I taped a workout video, just to show what was possible. Surprisingly, the video had over 10,000 hits in less than two months. People wrote to me: to say "thank you," for further encouragement in their own journeys and to request more videos. *Interested? Google "Heather Dugan," or "Eight Weeks on Crutches? Strategies for Success."*

4) Aim for Gratitude. If you're ever tempted to dip a toe into the pity pool, sit down and write yourself an email. Let your mind drift freely over what you *have* and list, item by item, your gratitudes. It may be as simple as sunshine, a good night's sleep, the fresh mango in your refrigerator or the positive impact you made by chatting with a grocery store clerk. But they all count. List your friends, your family. Be glad that there are people you can call on for help when you need it. While you're at it, think of whom you might be able to help, even in your less than stellar state with a simple email or phone call of encouragement.

There is *always* something to be thankful for. In finding it, you make no changes to your circumstance, but you may radically transform your own experience within it. My children have heard —many times— that if you wander a park looking for garbage, you will find it. But if you look for flowers, you will find them instead —in the same park! *What your heart seeks, your spirit will find.*

And consider this: Your body is healing. *You* will most likely end up far better than you were before your surgery. In my own case, my healing has been effected by the after-death gifts of others. Yes, my ankle reconstruction required tissue donation and bone grafts. When I considered the magnitude of *those* gifts, my little struggles seemed pretty insignificant. Complaining about my healing process sounded similar to a sick child whining about taking medication essential for restoring his health. In fact, I felt pretty damned lucky —and lacking in things to whine about. *You can read "Donating Dreams and Gifts of Life: Giving When it Hurts" in the additional reading at the end of this book.*

5) Simplify. Consider your recovery time to be a mini-vacation from your usual standards. You have a pass.

Use it. Avoid worrying about details you can't control and consider alternatives. For instance, my own surgical recovery coincided with the Christmas holidays. There was no reasonable way to do the usual baking, shopping and entertaining while on crutches —so I selected our favorite traditions and simplified.

To be honest, it was a great excuse. I'm a fan of simplification. Choosing the meaningful over obligatory time-fillers is a personal goal, and the crutches and cast gave me extra courage to opt for the easy.

Yes, I missed a few things, but they will be there next year if I want them. I chose the essentials —my family and my friends —and the holiday time proved to be even more special *because* it was stripped down to those core elements. The lack of embellishments actually allowed more of the underlying beauty to shine through.

6) Ramp up for rehab. Your doctor laid the groundwork for your healing. This casted time is an incubation period. Rest with purpose, because next comes the real work! It's essential to maintain as much of your fitness as possible during your cast time if maximum recovery is your goal. My therapists commented often on how far ahead I was simply because I'd continued doing whatever I could while living life on crutches. When it was time for my physical therapy, I was ready to go.

My last official therapy session was a week ago, but I've a list of daily exercises I continue to do —and will expand upon— in my quest to fully recover both strength and stability in my right ankle. I'm actually doing the exercises for *both* of my ankles now, as I want to equip myself for a long life rich with fulfilling activities and adventures.

Physical therapy —your rehabilitation— is, again, not something to simply "get through." It's an exposure of your weaknesses —but comes with a roadmap to overcome them. Inconsistency in doing your exercises cheats you in ways that will impact the rest of your life. No excuses here. They are mandatory unless you are OK with lowering your standard of life. Aim high to keep all of your options open.

Every runner knows that the *mental* component of conquering a steep hill requires as much strength and endurance as the physical. There is a significant performance difference for the athlete who pumps her arms and attacks the challenge versus the one who grimly plods on up the incline. My daughter's cross-country coach recognized the power of attitude by giving the girls another word for "hill." In high school, my daughter quit climbing hills and began running up "opportunities."

That's what this time of temporary challenge can and should be: an opportunity. Yes, few things will be "normal," and some of it will be hard. But, you can do this well by leaning into the "opportunity" of it all.

You'll get further and enjoy your life more by generating some personal momentum rather than dragging your heels.

There will be happy surprises wherein you find new strengths and abilities. You will achieve things in different ways and maybe even be a little proud of yourself. You will inspire others —*who's going to complain about being tired when they have you, schlepping alongside them, on crutches?* And your grin, as you conquer new challenges, will help others remember that their own lives contain possibilities.

Yes. You can do this. Six weeks, eight weeks, even a lifetime… You can't always change the timeframe of a challenge, but you can absolutely impact the overall experience with your own attitude. And when you do? Send me an email. Tell me about the mistakes, the surprises…

Tell me what *you* learned and what *you* achieved while stuffing mail down your pants and sandwiches down your shirt.

Stuffing Sandwiches Down My Shirt...

CHAPTER 7

"As I plucked up marbles with my toes and wobbled on my new right ankle, I had doubts as to whether these silly little exercises would do anything but amuse curious bystanders."

SIX MONTHS OFF THE NEW STARTING LINE

The view was spectacular, but the climb itself was my real milestone.

Six months after rediscovering my right ankle following its mandatory eight-week hibernation in a burgundy cast, I surveyed a stretch of the San Juan mountain range from atop Handies Peak, a 14,058 peak in southern Colorado. In the previous week, my daughter and I had trekked up and down rock strewn terrain, splashed across streams on wet rocks and precarious logs and shimmied up vertical climbs to alpine lakes and remote vistas found only by dedicated hikers and lucky little marmots.

The loose rocks and uneven surfaces kept me focused but grew my gratitude and confidence as I conquered each challenge.

Atop Handies Peak, I spun around slowly, surveying the panorama as if planted on my own personal Everest. The spectacular view and thin air were both cause for deep breaths.

"You got your life back."

No one heard me. No one needed to hear those words but me.

During my first physical therapy sessions, as I gingerly plucked up marbles with my toes and wobbled about on my new right ankle, I had doubts as to whether the "silly" little exercises would do anything but amuse curious bystanders. But it was my only shot. My therapists explained the process of strengthening essential muscles and rebuilding my balance. Over time, I began to grow cautious optimism.

"This is better than last time, isn't it?" My arms fluttered a little as I teetered on my right ankle, eyes focused on the room's exit sign. "I feel like a flamingo!"

Brittany checked her chart and nodded. "Much better! Now close your eyes." I wobbled wildly, planted both feet and sighed. Frustrated.

"It takes time. This is still early," she commented.

Gradually, I advanced to more difficult exercises and then began doing them on my own at my gym: stepping up and down off of weight benches, doing side squats with a red elastic band around my ankles, swinging my left foot into counterclockwise toe taps as I stood on my right —arms flung for better balance. As a preventative measure, I repeated every strength and balance-building exercise assigned to my right ankle on my left ankle as well.

"Aren't you the lady with the leg cast?" "Weren't you on crutches?" My advancement back into physical activity was an affirmative happy ending for those who had spotted me anywhere along the journey from injury to surgery to health —but for me, it was my new starting line with no finish in sight.

Surprisingly, a few weeks later my doctor approved me to run again —*"With moderation!"* I never expected that.

Stretching at a trailhead that same afternoon, unable to wait a moment more, I was afraid. Not of pain — which I have had an unfortunate tendency to ignore— but of disappointment. Could my ankle really do this? What about the rest of my body? I calculated that it had been over a year since I had last run.

But with those first gentle steps, I began building tentative trust in the essential joint that had failed me so miserably the previous spring. Half a mile in, I was relieved to find my cardio capacity still adequate (thanks to the workout workarounds I'd used while on crutches and in rehab), and after two miles more, I jogged off the trail in a happy sweat.

And a few short months later, my daughter and I headed back to Colorado for some intensive hiking that would fully test my ankle and my recovery.

Surprisingly, I instinctively miss the old crutches sometimes —they became an extension of my own body during my time of dependence. But those moments are fleeting, and hiking poles seem more than a fair trade.

And with my restored, renewed ankle, I again have the freedom to venture as far from paved paths into wilderness as my curiosity takes me, limited only by the length of lifetime left to me to enjoy.

* * * * *

MORE INSPIRATION

Stuffing Sandwiches Down My Shirt...

"It's so easy to invite people over when you can add, 'of course the house is a mess and I have no food... the crutches, you know...' It sets expectations to an attainable level."

SIX MORE UPSIDES TO MY DOWNTIME ON CRUTCHES

December 2012: As I sailed by Christmas shoppers at the mall last month, unencumbered by heavy bags (because my crutches provide the *perfect* excuse to travel lightly), I couldn't keep the smile off my face.

My November ankle surgery —two bone grafts and a ligament graft —capped a difficult year thick with tragedies, the most significant being the loss of my dear brother-in-law to cancer. Upon approach, the ankle surgery and recovery time looked to be but another challenging energy drainer.

But in "It's Not a Crutch if it Makes You Stronger: 8 Weeks, 9 Discoveries," I described some surprising upsides to my post-op downtime. And in late night TV "But wait, there's more!" fashion, I must share six additional benefits:

1) I've made new friends. At such an isolating time when one would logically expect a decreasing circle, mine actually grew. Odd. You'd think that labor-intensive friends like me (at present) would be less desirable —especially at grocery stores where I tend to bank bags of shredded cheese off of cart compatriots before actually achieving the basket. But somehow, I've been fortunate to forge some new and lasting relationships that grew quite simply from my "better than a puppy" leg cast. I cherish the old ones (think "tenure," not "wrinkles," ladies!) but am also grateful for these new friends in my life!

2) I've grown more flexible —and it's not *just* all that great physical stretching at the gym (which I highly recommend). As adults, we're used to setting our own schedules and having the ability to make random choices. Life is an endless menu —with options for selecting our "dressing on the side" and to "skip the croutons, please." It's easy to get picky and stuck in our tried and true ways. We close doors reflexively, often without thought to what we might be missing, in our rush to simplify choices.

Over these past few weeks, I've had the opportunity to slide into the lives of my friends. Yes, they're more than willing to build an errand run around *my* needs, but it's been enlightening to discover their own shortcuts and favorites. It's been good for me to get a text saying, "Heading out to shop in an hour. Wanna come?" and to change my plans to maximize the sudden "get out of the house" opportunity. It's funny that, when so much has been wrapped around my present needs, I've been more aware than ever that it's *not* all about me.

3) I'm even more spontaneous. It's so easy to invite people over when you can add, "of course the house is a mess and I have no food… the crutches, you know…" It sets expectations to an attainable level.

Not sure what I'll do when I'm walking and driving again. "I was on crutches for a while" won't fare better than a punch line in another month or so. So, I'll have to work on alternatives: "Oh no, we've been ransacked" might help with the occasional junk mail mess, but I'm not sure how I'll handle the non-cooking thing. With good carryout, I think… The point is my innate spontaneity has newly expanded boundaries. And since that increases "connection," that's a good thing.

4) I appreciate my health so very much. I did, and I do. Even more. My recovery has been easier because, except for the surgically enhanced ankle, I'm in great shape. Being temporarily stymied by a physical handicap builds my anticipation towards the day I can easily manage desired activities again. While I'm semi-impervious to pain, I'm not immune to injury. That knowledge makes me grateful for when my body works well —the same feeling that surged in me every time I ran a trail. *Wiggling (painted) toes in my cast as I type —how cool!*

5) I am physically stronger and mentally tougher. Besides the obvious muscles and core strength that good crutch use will build, I feel more capable mentally and emotionally. Once you have made breakfast, fed a dog and transported your laptop to the kitchen on one foot; recorded and sent audio to clients while hopping between mic and computer; written amusing insightful articles while undergoing a bone growth treatment, washed your hair in full arabesque (to elevate your foot) and chest-bumped a shopping cart through the grocery on crutches... Please. Give me a *real* challenge. My closest comparison would be navigating a mountain with a lawn mower assembly manual as the map. Written in Korean. But not a problem, I can do this. *You can too.*

But best of all, **6) I've inadvertently inspired others**. Since this is basically my life mission, I could probably rest here (but I won't). Connecting to others is the essential, critical element to life. Encouraging one another up the impossible cliff sides, applauding one another across finish lines and inspiring one another when we stand on the verge of greatness, failure or mediocrity... this is why we buy the popcorn! It's the climax, the epitome, the reason for putting warm feet on a cold floor in the morning. And my surgical setback has allowed me to help others step forward on their own journeys. Reader emails, random encounters and conversations, video subscribers... While I can't run an errand for anyone at present, I can still contribute something valuable. I think that's why I couldn't stop smiling at the mall last weekend. Well, that and the fact that I could play my crutch card and avoid all that frenetic shopping madness.

I feel a little sheepish for enjoying this experience, but what an excellent gift to connect with so many in such a positive way! And while I'm in no way angling for a repeat, based on my experience thus far, a zippered slip-on cast would be sooo helpful when dining without a reservation. In case you're wondering what to give me next Christmas.

"There is no 'gain' in premature worry. So many of our decisions are miles ahead. Setting them aside, temporarily, as calendar reminders givs us freedom to live more fully until actual choice is necessary."

THE CALENDAR CHECK

Sometimes a bad day turns into a bad week. Or a temporary challenge extends into an indefinite time frame. These are the times we're prone to deep sighing at stoplights —when we become aware that we are "making an effort" to stay positive and consciously throw back our shoulders. It's when Life shifts from pizza/movie nights to grueling "will I need a tissue?" endurance contests. Such challenges are generally unavoidable. However, we have options in how we choose to muscle through them, and before negative energy can ooze over *my* life like a dark cloud, I set up a *Calendar Check.*

Uncertain miseries —limitless tests of the spirit— are energy drains. Whether it's an unfulfilling job, a tenuous relationship or health difficulties, the indefinite aspect of any one of these can feel like an ongoing sprint with no finish line.

We *need* a finish line on our challenges! A mark to aim for, a date for the big exhale. Otherwise, a single stress can create an ongoing shallow breathing/shallow living experience in which we stew over decisions prematurely while waiting for an ending over which we have no control.

Having stewed myself into a mushy mess on more than one occasion, I recommend this better alternative.

Log in to your electronic calendar and go out a few weeks —or months. Write yourself a message: *"Is it better yet?" "Remember when you were worried about (fill in the blank)" "Are you closer to (fill in the dream)?"*

Consciously let go of whatever the brain-rubdown may be for this set period of time. Give yourself permission to let go and allow resolution to drift into view by setting a distant calendar reminder. If you're unsure of the adequate "pause" length on your dilemma, talk to a friend. They will, hopefully, be blunt with you. *"You want to give him another month? Give him a week and then move on."* Or *"You really think you'll get career direction in just a month? I'd wait six weeks. At least."*

Stop and think about all the time, energy and joy you've wasted worrying about a future choice. There is no "gain" in premature worry. So many of our decisions are miles ahead. Setting them aside, temporarily, as calendar reminders gives us freedom to live more fully until actual choice is necessary.

I remember getting one such reminder while hiking down a 14er in Colorado last June. It surprised me. It made me smile. It made me grateful for not wasting so many great days on a decision that didn't really need me after all.

It also helped me decide that calendar entries are a worthy means of delegation. I've already bookmarked a couple of decisions onto my 2013 calendar. And I'm already thanking myself profusely for giving *me* such a thoughtful gift.

"That these broken-hearted strangers retained the capacity to care for unknown others —this moves me."

DONATING DREAMS AND GIFTS OF LIFE: GIVING WHEN IT HURTS

I'm a future organ donor. The emblem is affixed to my driver's license, and I've discussed my intentions with family and friends. Can't say that I'm keeping the mileage down —my parts will be well worn by the time anyone gets them. *But the section of my brain that remembers where I've parked my car? Barely used at all...*

As a recent recipient of two bone grafts and a ligament graft, tissue and organ donations now carry a personal and sacred significance for me. I cringed before my ankle surgery, thinking of foreign matter fusing with my body —but *after* the essential surgery was completed, I cried, overcome by the magnitude of the gifts I'd been given.

It is likely, given the nature of my bone grafts, that grieving parents made the choice to enable my ankle reconstruction as they wrestled against the erasure of the ordinary family dreams we all cherish. I wonder how many other lives they changed on that dark and terrible day. *Did someone tell them that their gift might save eight lives and provide healing to fifty more*?* That these broken-hearted strangers retained the capacity to care for unknown others —this moves me.

My hospital folder held encoded donor family contact information. I've tapped out the beginnings of personal notes multiple times now. I begin to see faces reading my words, hit "delete" and try again. Grappling with words in the manner of a chef assembling his ingredients. Only simple words are needed. But knowing that my words will link to a critical chapter in the shortened life of someone's son or daughter, I'm measuring them carefully.

It is not lost on me that, just as a child's tissue donation is repairing my ankle and allowing me continued access to the adventurous life I love, my words may have a similar capacity to facilitate mending in a donor's family. Unexceptional words. *"I'm sorry."* *"Thank you."* But they matter. And just as acknowledgement is a critical step in moving through loss, gratitude is, likewise, essential to full appreciation of a gift. The words will come...

* If you haven't yet made your intention to be a tissue and organ donor official, please search for the "organ donor" website in your state or country.

Stuffing Sandwiches Down My Shirt...

"View yourself as a creative problem-solver with a new set of challenges to achieve."

LETTER: MY WHOLE LIFE IS CHANGING BECAUSE OF A STUPID BROKEN FOOT!

December 2012:

Hi there, my name is Amy.

I recently broke my foot in two places and I find out today if I will need surgery or can avoid it by just being in a cast and I am freaking out! You seem so sweet yet tough at the same time: a single mom with this injury, yet keeping your spirits high and going to the gym. I honestly have cried myself to sleep the last two nights and have been a depressed mess! I feel like my whole life is changing because of a stupid broken foot! I can't take the train to work, haven't left my apartment or worn anything besides shorts and pj's and feel gross. Hope to hear back from you.

Hi Amy,

I'm so glad you wrote. Discouragement is a lonely place to live for any amount of time, and this is an especially hard time of year to face such a challenge.

My ankle repair was considered a major surgical event and included two bone grafts and a ligament graft. The hospital staff reminded me numerous times that this recent surgery was a significantly bigger deal than my previous one. Anyone would be a little scared. I certainly was, and your fears are completely understandable.

Following my last ankle surgery, I had live-in help in the form of my now ex-husband. Facing a second surgery as a single and decade older single mom was daunting (!), but surprisingly, it has been much easier this time! The biggest game changer for me has been to face it as a challenge I can achieve rather than an ordeal to get through. It's similar to approaching a steep hill on a trail run: If you aim only to get up and over, you'll run out of steam, but if you attack the incline, you will almost always perform better.

It *will* be OK. Really! I'm amazed at how "OK" my own experience has been. It is critical, however, to find ways to 1) stay physically active, 2) be mentally engaged and 3) remain socially connected. We need these three components to function well when life is uncomplicated. They become even more important when we are challenged. Disconnecting on any of these key factors upsets our equilibrium and can start a depressive spiral.

Hopefully, you will be able to avoid the surgery. Regardless of that, while you are "one-footed," take these important first two steps:

• View yourself as a creative problem-solver with a new set of challenges to achieve.

• Make a list of your "human" resources and begin asking for help.

Once you're able to restore a little order into your days, allowing you to reinforce those three critical components (physical, mental and social), you'll have the necessary balance from which to turn this challenging "negative" into an opportunity for you to discover new strengths within yourself.

Please let me know how things go. I'm rooting for you.

~Heather

"Success or failure is simply information about the interaction of my abilities with circumstance and environment at a particular moment. It's changeable, and I can change it."

REFORMED GYM CLASS WALLFLOWER: CREATING ACHIEVEMENT OPPORTUNITIES INSTEAD OF EXCUSES

January 2013: Oddly, now that I'm waddling about in a walking boot rather than swinging along gracefully on crutches in a leg cast, I blend in a little better at the gym. Doing pull-ups in my burgundy cast took a lot more confidence than I ever had in my former life as a gym class wallflower when my dominant desire was not to be noticed. Back in high school, my cast would have been a *great* excuse to hide in a corner with a book. Thankfully, *this* wallflower got legs.

I don't get quite as many offers of help now—which is fine— I'm pretty capable except for occasional wobbles on this round-bottomed surgical boot I'm wearing. I *do* get a lot of comments on my "dedication," however, and feel compelled to explain that it's not so much about commitment as it is a simple, selfish desire to feel my best and get out of the house.

Accomplishing my normal tasks on crutches or one foot effectively blended regular and intense exercise into my day-to-day living. Just getting breakfast for me and the dog was a pretty intense workout. The gym? That was just for fun.

You see, several years ago I recognized that the "gym class wallflower" I once was had missed out on a lot. Perfectionism, fear of failure or a plain old lack of confidence? It was probably an unlovely blend of all three that prevented me from trying new things and enjoying physical challenges. But it was like waiting to live until no one was looking. Now? I *always* like to try. Success or failure is simply information about the interaction of my abilities with circumstance and environment at a particular moment. It's changeable, and I can change it. Knowing this alleviates the pressure and amps up the fun.

The best thing about approaching life with a "let's see what I can do" attitude is that it tends to pull others along to a higher level too. When I step up to the pull up bar, whether in a cast, walking boot or, someday soon, in a running shoe again, I'm rarely alone for long. I like to think the mental head talk goes like this: "If *she* (a 5'4", 110 lb woman) can do pull ups, I *know* I can!

And yes. You can.

ABOUT THE AUTHOR

Heather Dugan is a nationally published writer/advice columnist/author and voiceover/video talent and producer who most frequently covers business, relationship, fitness and travel topics. A dedicated traveler and life-balance advocate, Heather is also a savvy speaker and spokesperson, a skilled communicator who can educate and inspire with a twist of humor.

You may have heard Heather in radio/TV ads, eLearning and corporate videos or as an annoying phone voice informing you that you've misdialed. Heather enjoys connecting with readers via social media and by email at her website, www.heatherdugan.com, where you will also find links to other articles, books, voiceovers and videos. She resides in Central Ohio with her children and a wayward chocolate lab, is slightly addicted to outdoor activities and would never let her passport expire. In between deodorizing shin guards, power grocery shopping and explaining proper application of lawn care products in corporate videos, her passion for travel and the great outdoors takes her off the map (*oops!*) and all over the world. She considers humor to be her best accessory.

Thanks for reading! Don't be a stranger. Find me on Twitter, LinkedIn, YouTube and Facebook. Subscribe to my website (www.heatherdugan.com) for book updates, videos and tips to building a genuine, balanced life.

~Heather

Stuffing Sandwiches Down My Shirt...

OTHER BOOKS:

Pickup in Aisle Twelve (Angie Wharton series, Book 1): After a would-be suitor tails her to a grocery store checkout, Angie Wharton confronts the grim realities of her post-divorce dating options. Niggling guilt, a fickle resolve and easy access to her sister's dinner table have kept her on the sidelines, but her brother-in-law's patience --and supplies of cabernet are running low.

Pressed into posting an online dating profile, Angie decides to take the offense before love passes her by. But navigating this virtual world of blurred photos and lonely hearts will require her to create both a roadmap and a new understanding of herself.

Lipstick? Check. Eye contact? More or less. Awkward moments? Uh huh. *Love...?*

Download at Amazon, Barnes and Noble, the iBookstore and at www.heatherdugan.com.

REVIEWS:

Funny and wise! "...Heather Dugan does a great job of being wryly funny, while poking fun of the pitfalls and awkward situations involved in this shark —and quirky —guy-infested world of online and blind dating. Her insight expands into family relationships and is quite poignant at times..."

A great read —even for guys! "Heather Dugan has done an outstanding job of capturing some of the choices, challenges and even occasional humor of life after divorce in the age of digital dating. You will root for Angie to find the right person, and her journey offers fresh insights into the Mars and Venus worlds in which men and women often orbit."

Surprise Discovery! "...the fact that she conveys all this with side-splitting laughter is just a "cake frosting" bonus. Now I have to ask myself if I was seen as a produce aisle stalker. If you've ever online dated this is a must read to self-assess and have a few kicks at your own expense. There's now a new "Angie's List". Ms Dugan... More please..."

Walking the Aisles with Angie... "From the gut, the heart and a sophisticated but down-to-earth funny bone, this book is truly a page-turner. I felt like I was with Angie as she walked down grocery aisles, as she walked alone into restaurants, and as she faced surprises, pleasant and unpleasant. Heather Dugan promises more in the Angie Wharton Series...

COMING SOON...

In **"Profile on Page Nine,"** the second book of the Angie Wharton series (**"Pickup in Aisle Twelve"**), Angie finds no strength in numbers as her newly single sister Katie launches forward with a firm belief in pushup bras and payback. With a firm grip on hope and a shoulder shrug towards the past, Angie strives to lead them both through the perils and pitfalls of midlife dating toward, hopefully, the temptations of second chance love.

"Date Like a Grown-Up: Anecdotes, Admissions of Guilt and Advice Between Friends" examines both the bad and the lucky choices of women in their second single lives. With at least half of the adult population attempting a "do-over" on their most committed relationships and many getting it wrong yet a second time, these proven "do's and don'ts" are first date gold for women navigating midlife dating, insightful revelations for the men who would date them and vicarious entertainment for thankful sideline observers. Topics include effective filtering, taking online dating "off-net" and strategically building a larger social network. Engaging narratives such as "Parking Lot Apology," "The Percocet Proposal" and "Wednesdays and Every Other Weekend" provide the punctuating proof for specific dating principals outlined in the book.